ANDREW JOHNSON

Megan M. Gunderson

Checkerboard
Library

An Imprint of Abdo Publishing
abdobooks.com

ABDOBOOKS.COM

Published by Abdo Publishing, a division of ABDO, PO Box 398166, Minneapolis, Minnesota 55439. Copyright © 2021 by Abdo Consulting Group, Inc. International copyrights reserved in all countries. No part of this book may be reproduced in any form without written permission from the publisher. Checkerboard Library™ is a trademark and logo of Abdo Publishing.

Printed in the United States of America, North Mankato, Minnesota
052020
092020

THIS BOOK CONTAINS
RECYCLED MATERIALS

Design: Emily O'Malley, Kelly Doudna, Mighty Media, Inc.
Production: Mighty Media, Inc.
Editor: Liz Salzmann

Cover Photograph: Library of Congress
Interior Photographs: Albert de Bruijn/iStockphoto, p. 37; American School/Getty Images, p. 21; AP Images, pp. 6 (birthplace), 11, 36; Jeff Greenberg/Alamy, pp. 13, 33; Library of Congress, pp. 6 (portrait), 7 (portrait), 17, 18, 23, 25, 30, 31, 40; Library of Congress/Getty Images, p. 5; Mathew Brady/Getty Images, p. 28; MPI/Getty Images, p. 15; National Archives, pp. 7, 19, 29; National Park Service, pp. 6 (Eliza Johnson), 14; Pete Souza/Flickr, p. 44; Shutterstock Images, pp. 6, 32, 38, 39; Time Life Pictures/Getty Images, p. 27; Wikimedia Commons, pp. 22, 40 (George Washington), 42

Library of Congress Control Number: 2019956430

Publisher's Cataloging-in-Publication Data
Names: Gunderson, Megan M., author.
Title: Andrew Johnson / by Megan M. Gunderson
Description: Minneapolis, Minnesota : Abdo Publishing, 2021 | Series: The United States presidents | Includes online resources and index.
Identifiers: ISBN 9781532193590 (lib. bdg.) | ISBN 9781098212230 (ebook)
Subjects: LCSH: Johnson, Andrew, 1808-1875--Juvenile literature. | Presidents--Biography--Juvenile literature. | Presidents--United States--History--Juvenile literature. | Legislators--United States—Biography--Juvenile literature. | Politics and government--Biography--Juvenile literature.
Classification: DDC 973.81092--dc23

★ CONTENTS ★

Andrew Johnson

Andrew Johnson was the seventeenth president of the United States. He had become Abraham Lincoln's vice president in March 1865. The next month, Lincoln was **assassinated**. Johnson then became president.

Johnson tried to follow the rules of the US **Constitution**. He favored states' rights over increasing the power of the federal government. Because of this, President Johnson and Congress often disagreed. They argued about how to run the country after the war.

While president, Johnson challenged a law Congress had passed. Congress felt he had broken the law. So in 1868, Johnson became the first president to be **impeached**. The Senate voted to decide if he should be removed from office. By just one vote, the Senate decided to keep Johnson in office.

Johnson was not nominated for a second term. After leaving office, he became the only former president elected to the US Senate. Johnson had a difficult presidency. Yet he was a lifelong politician who always fought hard for his beliefs.

Andrew Johnson

TIMELINE ★

1827

On May 17, Johnson married Eliza McCardle.

1835

Johnson began serving in the Tennessee House of Representatives.

1843

Johnson began serving in the US House of Representatives.

1853

Johnson became governor of Tennessee.

1808

On December 29, Andrew Johnson was born in Raleigh, North Carolina.

1829

In Tennessee, Johnson was elected to the Greeneville town council.

1841

Johnson was elected to the Tennessee state senate.

1857

Johnson began serving in the US Senate.

1864

Johnson was elected vice president under Lincoln.

1875

Johnson was elected to the US Senate. On July 31, Andrew Johnson died.

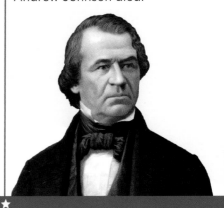

1865

The Civil War ended on April 9. On April 15, President Lincoln died. That day, Johnson became the seventeenth US president. Johnson announced his Reconstruction plans.

1861

The American Civil War began on April 12. On June 8, Tennessee voted to secede.

1862

President Abraham Lincoln appointed Johnson military governor of Tennessee. The Homestead Act passed.

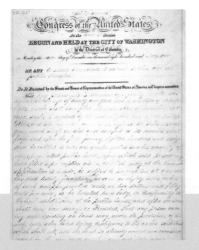

1868

The US House of Representatives impeached President Johnson, but the Senate voted to keep him in office.

1867

Congress passed the Tenure of Office Act. Nebraska became the thirty-seventh US state.

"The life of a republic lies certainly in **the energy, virtue, and intelligence** of its citizens."

ANDREW JOHNSON

DID YOU KNOW?

- ★ Legend has it that Eliza McCardle fell in love with Andrew Johnson at first sight. When she saw him arrive in Greeneville, Tennessee, she told her friends, "There goes my beau, girls." She had not even met him yet! But soon after, they fell in love and married.

- ★ While Johnson was president, the United States purchased what would become Alaska. They paid Russia just over seven million dollars for the land. That is just two cents per acre!

- ★ When former president Johnson returned to the Senate, he was welcomed with a bouquet of flowers on his desk.

- ★ In 1868, Johnson became the first of three US presidents to be impeached. The other two are Bill Clinton in 1998 and Donald Trump in 2019.

Young Andrew

Andrew Johnson was born on December 29, 1808, in Raleigh, North Carolina. Andrew had an older brother named William. His older sister, Elizabeth, died in childhood.

Their father, Jacob, had various jobs. He worked at an inn and a bank. He was also the town bell ringer. Their mother, Mary "Polly" McDonough, was a weaver. Still, the family was poor.

When Andrew was just three, his father died. Jacob had jumped into a pond to save three men from drowning. The incident weakened him, and he died in January 1812. Later, Andrew's mother remarried.

Growing up, Andrew enjoyed playing ball, swimming, and fishing. He also was very interested in learning. However, his family could not afford to send him to school. So, he and his brother soon became **apprentices.**

FAST FACTS

BORN: December 29, 1808

WIFE: Eliza McCardle (1810–1876)

CHILDREN: 5

POLITICAL PARTY: Democrat

AGE AT INAUGURATION: 56

YEARS SERVED: 1865–1869

VICE PRESIDENT: none

DIED: July 31, 1875, age 66

Andrew's birthplace is now part of Moredecai Historic Park in Raleigh.

Tailor's Apprentice

When Andrew was 14, he became a tailor's **apprentice**. Andrew's contract said he would work for James J. Selby until he was 21. William was also Selby's apprentice.

At Selby's, Andrew became known for his interest in learning. He learned to read. And, he enjoyed listening to visitors discuss politics. A local man often read out loud as Andrew worked. The man read from a book of speeches by American and English **statesmen**. He later gave the book to Andrew. Andrew kept it for the rest of his life.

When Andrew was 15, he ran away from his job. Selby offered a ten dollar reward for his return. Andrew traveled from town to town. He worked for tailors in Carthage, North Carolina, and Laurens, South Carolina. But no one was supposed to hire a runaway apprentice. Andrew was always in danger of being caught.

Eventually, Andrew returned home to Raleigh. Without a large payment, Selby refused to release him from his contract. Andrew could not afford to buy his freedom. So, he decided to leave North Carolina. In 1826, Andrew moved to Greeneville, Tennessee.

After Johnson became president,
he claimed he could still sew a coat!

Family and Work

In Greeneville, Johnson opened his own tailor shop. He was a good tailor. Many people came to see him. They often discussed politics. Johnson met Eliza McCardle soon after arriving in Greeneville. They married the next year, on May 17, 1827.

Eliza Johnson attended school at the Rhea Academy in Greeneville.

The Johnsons had five children. They were named Martha, Charles, Mary, Robert, and Andrew. Mrs. Johnson read to her husband while he worked. She helped him improve his reading and writing skills. Johnson also studied the US **Constitution**.

Johnson became a good speaker. He loved **debating**. In fact, he joined debating societies at two nearby colleges. Johnson stood out as a leader in the town. He soon decided to become involved in politics.

Johnson led many political discussions at his tailor shop.

Tennessee Politician

In 1829, Johnson was elected to the Greeneville Town Council. On the council, he represented working-class people. Soon, Johnson was elected mayor of Greeneville.

Next, Johnson was elected to the Tennessee House of Representatives. As a **Democrat**, he served from 1835 to 1837. He served again from 1839 to 1841.

Congressman Johnson became known for his energetic speeches and his support of laborers. He voted against expanding railroads. He felt they harmed inns and other businesses. Johnson also fought wasteful government spending. In 1841, Johnson was elected to the Tennessee state senate.

Johnson was elected to the US House of Representatives in 1843. There, Johnson introduced a homestead bill. The bill would have given land in the West to settlers for free. However, Southern politicians defeated the bill. They feared it would reduce government earnings from land sales.

Johnson also favored states' rights. So, he supported the Compromise of 1850. Part of the compromise allowed certain new states to decide if they would allow slavery.

Johnson's excellent public speaking skills
helped him succeed in politics.

In 1853, Johnson became governor of Tennessee. He was reelected in 1855. As governor, Johnson helped improve the public school system. He also became a member of the state's new Agricultural Bureau. In this way, he continued helping farmers.

Loyal Senator

Johnson continued his political career. In 1857, he became a US senator. By now, slavery had become a major issue in the United States. Northerners wanted to end it. But Southerners wanted to keep it. As a senator, Johnson continued to support a state's right to allow slavery.

In November 1860, Abraham Lincoln was elected president. The Southern states feared President Lincoln would not support their right to own slaves. So a few weeks later, Southern states began **seceding**. They formed a new country called the Confederate States of America.

Abraham Lincoln

Johnson was a Southerner and a slave owner. However, he was against **secession**. He soon became the only Southern senator to remain in the US Senate. There, he kept fighting for his homestead bill. Southern politicians were no longer there to oppose it. So in 1862, the Homestead Act finally became law.

Meanwhile, the American **Civil War** began on April 12, 1861. On June 8, Tennessee voted to join the Confederacy. Johnson's family was then forced from his Tennessee home. The Confederates seized Johnson's property. The states that remained in the United States were now called the Union. Eventually, the Union began regaining control of Tennessee.

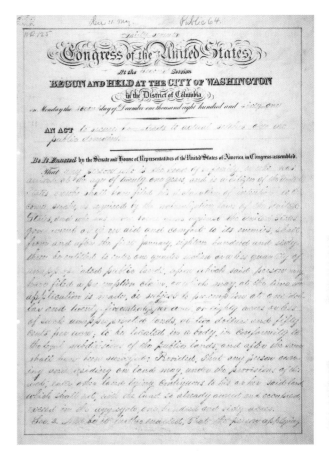

President Lincoln approved the Homestead Act on May 20, 1862.

In March 1862, President Lincoln made Johnson the military governor of Tennessee. Johnson's job was to help Tennessee rejoin the Union. He moved to Nashville, where his family joined him.

As governor, Johnson took control of Tennessee's railroads. He had people arrested for not supporting the federal government. Johnson also closed anti-Union newspapers.

In 1864, Johnson was chosen to run as Lincoln's vice president. Lincoln was a **Republican**. He wanted a loyal **Democrat** as his **running mate**. This helped show people that the national government represented everyone.

The Democrats nominated General George B. McClellan. His running mate was Representative George H. Pendleton. Running as the Union Party, Lincoln and Johnson easily defeated their opponents. They received 212 electoral votes. McClellan and Pendleton received just 21!

On April 9, 1865, the South surrendered. The North had won the **Civil War**. Yet before the country could begin healing, tragedy struck. On April 14, 1865, actor John Wilkes Booth shot President Lincoln. He wanted to avenge the South. Abraham Lincoln died the next day. A few hours later, Johnson was sworn in as president.

UNION NOMINATION

FOR PRESIDENT,

Abraham Lincoln
OF ILLINOIS.

FOR VICE PRESIDENT,

Andrew Johnson
OF TENNESSEE.

Lincoln and Johnson defeated McClellan and Pendleton by more than 400,000 popular votes.

7

Reconstruction

President Johnson and Congress now faced a difficult task. They had to bring the Southern states back into the Union. This is called Reconstruction.

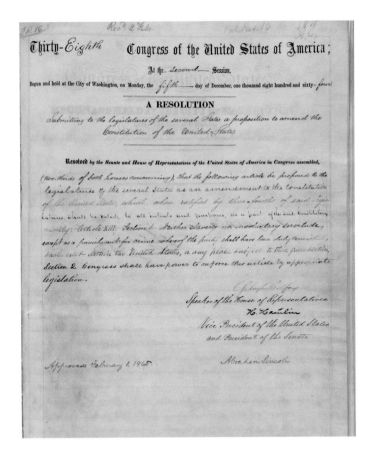

The Thirteenth Amendment

Johnson soon announced his plans for an easy, smooth reunion. Each Southern state could return if it wrote a new state **constitution** that banned slavery. And each state had to approve the Thirteenth **Amendment**. This also banned slavery. Each state also had to formally withdraw its act of **secession**. In addition, Southerners had to swear an oath of loyalty to the United States.

By December 1865, nearly every Southern state had completed Johnson's requirements. However, many Southern leaders now passed laws called black codes. Each state's codes were slightly different. Yet all black codes limited the rights of **freedmen**. They could not have skilled jobs or attend state schools. They could not own property or weapons, either.

Many Northern congressmen were against Johnson's

——— Thaddeus Stevens was one ———
of the congressmen who
worked to change Johnson's
Reconstruction policies.

Reconstruction plans and the black codes. So in 1866 and 1868, Congress voted to extend the Freedmen's Bureau.

Congress had formed this organization before the **Civil War** had ended. It provided freed slaves with food, medicine, and education. It also helped them settle on land in the South.

In 1866, Congress also passed the **Civil Rights** Act. This law defined US citizens as anyone born in the United States. It gave **freedmen** the right to own land and testify in court. President Johnson **vetoed** the Freedmen's Bureau and the Civil Rights Act. He felt they violated states' rights. However, Congress then voted against the presidential vetoes. Both acts became law.

Congress then protected the Civil Rights Act with a new **amendment**. The Fourteenth Amendment made all former slaves US citizens. Johnson fought the amendment, but Congress passed it anyway.

In 1867, Congress passed a series of Reconstruction Acts. New Southern state governments had to be formed. Southern states had to approve state **constitutions**. These had to guarantee voting rights for all men. The states also had to approve the Fourteenth Amendment. Afterward, Congress would let them rejoin the Union.

Congress passed its series of Reconstruction Acts
even though Johnson had vetoed them.

PRESIDENT JOHNSON'S CABINET

ONE TERM

April 15, 1865–March 4, 1869

- ★ **STATE:** William H. Seward
- ★ **TREASURY:** Hugh McCulloch
- ★ **WAR:** Edwin M. Stanton
  John M. Schofield (from June 1, 1868)
- ★ **NAVY:** Gideon Welles
- ★ **ATTORNEY GENERAL:** James Speed
  Henry Stanbery (from July 23, 1866)
  William M. Evarts (from July 20, 1868)
- ★ **INTERIOR:** John P. Usher
  James Harlan (from May 15, 1865)
  Orville H. Browning (from September 1, 1866)

President Andrew Johnson

8

Impeachment

Republican congressmen feared President Johnson would interfere with their Reconstruction plans. So on March 2, 1867, Congress passed the Tenure of Office Act. Now, anyone the Senate approved for office could not be removed from office without Senate approval. The act would stop Johnson from firing Republican supporters. This included **Secretary of War** Edwin M. Stanton.

Johnson **vetoed** this bill. He felt it gave Congress too much power over the president. But Congress voted against the veto. The Tenure of Office Act became law. President Johnson felt

Edwin M. Stanton served in the cabinets of three presidents. They were James Buchanan, Abraham Lincoln, and Andrew Johnson.

Today, Johnson's Greeneville home is part of the Andrew Johnson National Historic Site.

BRANCHES OF GOVERNMENT

The US government is divided into three branches. They are the executive, legislative, and judicial branches. This division is called a separation of powers. Each branch has some power over the others. This is called a system of checks and balances.

★ EXECUTIVE BRANCH

The executive branch enforces laws. It is made up of the president, the vice president, and the president's cabinet. The president represents the United States around the world. He or she oversees relations with other countries and signs treaties. The president signs bills into law and appoints officials and federal judges. He or she also leads the military and manages government workers.

★ LEGISLATIVE BRANCH

The legislative branch makes laws, maintains the military, and regulates trade. It also has the power to declare war. This branch consists of the Senate and the House of Representatives. Together, these two houses make up Congress. Each state has two senators. A state's population determines the number of representatives it has.

★ JUDICIAL BRANCH

The judicial branch interprets laws. It consists of district courts, courts of appeals, and the Supreme Court. District courts try cases. If a person disagrees with a trial's outcome, he or she may appeal. If a court of appeals supports the ruling, a person may appeal to the Supreme Court. The Supreme Court also makes sure that laws follow the US Constitution.

THE PRESIDENT ★

★ QUALIFICATIONS FOR OFFICE

To be president, a person must meet three requirements. A candidate must be at least 35 years old and a natural-born US citizen. He or she must also have lived in the United States for at least 14 years.

★ ELECTORAL COLLEGE

The US presidential election is an indirect election. Voters from each state choose electors to represent them in the Electoral College. The number of electors from each state is based on the state's population. Each elector has one electoral vote. Electors are pledged to cast their vote for the candidate who receives the highest number of popular votes in their state. A candidate must receive the majority of Electoral College votes to win.

★ TERM OF OFFICE

Each president may be elected to two four-year terms. Sometimes, a president may only be elected once. This happens if he or she served more than two years of the previous president's term.

The presidential election is held on the Tuesday after the first Monday in November. The president is sworn in on January 20 of the following year. At that time, he or she takes the oath of office:

> *I do solemnly swear (or affirm) that I will faithfully execute the office of President of the United States, and will to the best of my ability, preserve, protect and defend the Constitution of the United States.*

LINE OF SUCCESSION

The Presidential Succession Act of 1947 defines who becomes president if the president cannot serve. The vice president is first in the line of succession. Next are the Speaker of the House and the President Pro Tempore of the Senate. If none of these individuals is able to serve, the office falls to the president's cabinet members. They would take office in the order in which each department was created:

Secretary of State

Secretary of the Treasury

Secretary of Defense

Attorney General

Secretary of the Interior

Secretary of Agriculture

Secretary of Commerce

Secretary of Labor

Secretary of Health and Human Services

Secretary of Housing and Urban Development

Secretary of Transportation

Secretary of Energy

Secretary of Education

Secretary of Veterans Affairs

Secretary of Homeland Security

While in office, the president receives a salary of $400,000 each year. He or she lives in the White House and has 24-hour Secret Service protection.

The president may travel on a Boeing 747 jet called Air Force One. The airplane can accommodate 76 passengers. It has kitchens, a dining room, sleeping areas, and a conference room. It also has fully equipped offices with the latest communications systems. Air Force One can fly halfway around the world before needing to refuel. It can even refuel in flight!

Air Force One

If the president wishes to travel by car, he or she uses Cadillac One. It has been modified with heavy armor and communications systems. The president takes

star star star

Cadillac One

Cadillac One along when visiting other countries if secure transportation will be needed.

The president also travels on a helicopter called Marine One. Like the presidential car, Marine One accompanies the president when traveling abroad if necessary.

Sometimes, the president needs to get away and relax with family and friends. Camp David is the official presidential retreat. It is located in the cool, wooded mountains of Maryland. The US Navy maintains the retreat, and the US Marine Corps keeps it secure. The camp offers swimming, tennis, golf, and hiking.

When the president leaves office, he or she receives lifetime Secret Service protection. He or she also receives a yearly pension of $207,800 and funding for office space, supplies, and staff.

Marine One

George Washington

Abraham Lincoln

Theodore Roosevelt

	PRESIDENT	PARTY	TOOK OFFICE
1	George Washington	None	April 30, 1789
2	John Adams	Federalist	March 4, 1797
3	Thomas Jefferson	Democratic-Republican	March 4, 1801
4	James Madison	Democratic-Republican	March 4, 1809
5	James Monroe	Democratic-Republican	March 4, 1817
6	John Quincy Adams	Democratic-Republican	March 4, 1825
7	Andrew Jackson	Democrat	March 4, 1829
8	Martin Van Buren	Democrat	March 4, 1837
9	William H. Harrison	Whig	March 4, 1841
10	John Tyler	Whig	April 6, 1841
11	James K. Polk	Democrat	March 4, 1845
12	Zachary Taylor	Whig	March 5, 1849
13	Millard Fillmore	Whig	July 10, 1850
14	Franklin Pierce	Democrat	March 4, 1853
15	James Buchanan	Democrat	March 4, 1857
16	Abraham Lincoln	Republican	March 4, 1861
17	Andrew Johnson	Democrat	April 15, 1865
18	Ulysses S. Grant	Republican	March 4, 1869
19	Rutherford B. Hayes	Republican	March 3, 1877

THEIR TERMS ★

LEFT OFFICE	TERMS SERVED	VICE PRESIDENT
March 4, 1797	Two	John Adams
March 4, 1801	One	Thomas Jefferson
March 4, 1809	Two	Aaron Burr, George Clinton
March 4, 1817	Two	George Clinton, Elbridge Gerry
March 4, 1825	Two	Daniel D. Tompkins
March 4, 1829	One	John C. Calhoun
March 4, 1837	Two	John C. Calhoun, Martin Van Buren
March 4, 1841	One	Richard M. Johnson
April 4, 1841	Died During First Term	John Tyler
March 4, 1845	Completed Harrison's Term	Office Vacant
March 4, 1849	One	George M. Dallas
July 9, 1850	Died During First Term	Millard Fillmore
March 4, 1853	Completed Taylor's Term	Office Vacant
March 4, 1857	One	William R.D. King
March 4, 1861	One	John C. Breckinridge
April 15, 1865	Served One Term, Died During Second Term	Hannibal Hamlin, Andrew Johnson
March 4, 1869	Completed Lincoln's Second Term	Office Vacant
March 4, 1877	Two	Schuyler Colfax, Henry Wilson
March 4, 1881	One	William A. Wheeler

Franklin D. Roosevelt

John F. Kennedy

Ronald Reagan

	PRESIDENT	PARTY	TOOK OFFICE
20	James A. Garfield	Republican	March 4, 1881
21	Chester Arthur	Republican	September 20, 1881
22	Grover Cleveland	Democrat	March 4, 1885
23	Benjamin Harrison	Republican	March 4, 1889
24	Grover Cleveland	Democrat	March 4, 1893
25	William McKinley	Republican	March 4, 1897
26	Theodore Roosevelt	Republican	September 14, 1901
27	William Taft	Republican	March 4, 1909
28	Woodrow Wilson	Democrat	March 4, 1913
29	Warren G. Harding	Republican	March 4, 1921
30	Calvin Coolidge	Republican	August 3, 1923
31	Herbert Hoover	Republican	March 4, 1929
32	Franklin D. Roosevelt	Democrat	March 4, 1933
33	Harry S. Truman	Democrat	April 12, 1945
34	Dwight D. Eisenhower	Republican	January 20, 1953
35	John F. Kennedy	Democrat	January 20, 1961

LEFT OFFICE	TERMS SERVED	VICE PRESIDENT
September 19, 1881	Died During First Term	Chester Arthur
March 4, 1885	Completed Garfield's Term	Office Vacant
March 4, 1889	One	Thomas A. Hendricks
March 4, 1893	One	Levi P. Morton
March 4, 1897	One	Adlai E. Stevenson
September 14, 1901	Served One Term, Died During Second Term	Garret A. Hobart, Theodore Roosevelt
March 4, 1909	Completed McKinley's Second Term, Served One Term	Office Vacant, Charles Fairbanks
March 4, 1913	One	James S. Sherman
March 4, 1921	Two	Thomas R. Marshall
August 2, 1923	Died During First Term	Calvin Coolidge
March 4, 1929	Completed Harding's Term, Served One Term	Office Vacant, Charles Dawes
March 4, 1933	One	Charles Curtis
April 12, 1945	Served Three Terms, Died During Fourth Term	John Nance Garner, Henry A. Wallace, Harry S. Truman
January 20, 1953	Completed Roosevelt's Fourth Term, Served One Term	Office Vacant, Alben Barkley
January 20, 1961	Two	Richard Nixon
November 22, 1963	Died During First Term	Lyndon B. Johnson

	PRESIDENT	PARTY	TOOK OFFICE
36	Lyndon B. Johnson	Democrat	November 22, 1963
37	Richard Nixon	Republican	January 20, 1969
38	Gerald Ford	Republican	August 9, 1974
39	Jimmy Carter	Democrat	January 20, 1977
40	Ronald Reagan	Republican	January 20, 1981
41	George H.W. Bush	Republican	January 20, 1989
42	Bill Clinton	Democrat	January 20, 1993
43	George W. Bush	Republican	January 20, 2001
44	Barack Obama	Democrat	January 20, 2009
45	Donald Trump	Republican	January 20, 2017

Barack Obama

★ PRESIDENTS MATH GAME ★

Have fun with this presidents math game! First, study the list above and memorize each president's name and number. Then, use math to figure out which president completes each equation below.

1. Bill Clinton − Andrew Johnson = ?

2. Harry S. Truman − Andrew Johnson = ?

3. Andrew Johnson + James Monroe = ?

Answers: 1. William McKinley (42 − 17 = 25)
2. Abraham Lincoln (33 − 17 = 16)
3. Grover Cleveland (17 + 5 = 22)